Action at a Distance

Action at a Distance
Christopher Petruccelli

Etchings Press
Indianapolis, Indiana

Copyright© 2014 by Christopher Petruccelli

This publication is made possible by funding provided by the College of Arts and Sciences and the English Department at the University of Indianapolis. Special thanks to IngramSpark and to those students who judged, edited, designed, and published this chapbook: Alyssa Kauffman, Ryan Plummer, Mirna Palacia Ornelas, and Tierney Bailey.

UNIVERSITY *of* INDIANAPOLIS.

Published by Etchings Press
1400 E. Hanna Ave.
Indianapolis, Indiana 46227
All rights reserved

etchings.uindy.edu
www.uindy.edu/cas/english

Printed by IngramSpark
ingramspark.com

Published in the United States of America

ISBN 978-0-9903475-9-0

23 22 21 20 19 18 17 16 15 14   2 3 4
Second Printing, 2019

Table of Contents

Malachite	1
Expectations of a Greyhound Bus Ride	2
October 2010	3
Morphology	4
Amos Montague Speaks to Mary Jane Capulet	5
Field Work	6
What Bothers Me About Us	7
Imagine if Eve Knew How to Bake	8
Probabilities	9
Ode to Mags	10
Imaginary Waltz with a Woman Wearing a Dress of Virga	11
Arrival of the Normandy Train	12
Eulogy for an Imagined Woman	13
Surviving Tennessee Heat	14
A Night With Marlowe's Love	15
What West May Be	16
The Last Night I Was the Person I Thought I Had Always Wanted to Be	17
Acknowledgments	19

Malachite

I carry her away in photons
that rest in my palms no more
than a second before they are cold
blue like old CSX trains.

The rail yard runs the length
of downtown Corbin,
153 miles from Greeneville,
but close enough that thunder
in one town whispers a cold front
to the other.

Tracks in Greene county
run through Whitley,
and I've been meaning to leave
this town for years now,
but I can't seem to hold
on long enough to climb
into cool beds of coal cars.

Expectations of a Greyhound Bus Ride

St. Louis rises from corn,
each building, shucked of its husk,
is carved from Missouri Meerschaum.
Stepping off the bus I walk into your chest—
three months and fifteen hours feels like
three months and fifteen hours.

    You whisper,

> *Coffee,*
> *is shit*
> *in the Midwest. They're too*
> *caught*
> *up in cattle and corn. The delicacy*
> *is doughnut ice cream sandwiches.*

In the Broadway Diner,
your hand crawls over unbleached
napkins to beaded water.
Flush lips pressing to cool glass,
we go to your room—the hunger for touch insatiable.

October 2010

I-95

The lemons were gone as soon as Morristown. Down the coast your McIntosh hair braided, unwashed had a scent as if it had gone brown. Chests became pillows, bodies were blankets, everything for weeks was biological. Burbank Ave stuck to the fabric as a reminder of Connecticut rain.

I-65

Bowling Green smelled like your hometown—goldenrod and coal. Here you were a stranger. Your knees bent like drinking straws and hard use wore your feet red with clay. A few days in the country reminded us of early American history, all cider and tobacco.

Route 63

The road foams at the sides of its mouth, frost rises early in the fall. Streets in Missouri begin teething as ice cuts coarse smiles into asphalt. Fields once green now lakes of hot mud.

US-25E

Through Cumberland Gap and at Bean Station, the white oaks weren't dying but going dormant. Hands at ten and two, you kept your distance in fear that sleep spores were contagious. In Tennessee, the sound of 23 strings came straight from the hills. The highway wound the mountains like the whorls of fingers.

Morphology

Scored phloem of sugar maple is sweet,
bright cambium fresh dead,
the borer drips clean syrup.
Around you, fainted samaras
rest in beds of snow and mud,
golden color lost among
russet slush.

I feel your muscles contract
to the cool bend of my hand curving
the arc of your waist.
Our feet push snow to banks,
the staggered bark of pines,
ground drunk with footsteps.

It was our first time,
hands full of each other,
necks crawling with breath,
clothes folding like anticlines.

Amos Montague Speaks to Mary Jane Capulet

The hoecakes start pale in the pan and turn a golden brown once the fire is more than kindling and tinder. The moon does not shine like polished silver or like a pale beauty in the window looking east—it glooms like a blemish, a shameful off-white aria. It is a white-bright blotch—stilled by broken spokes and axles. Morning starts with the choke like call of the cockerel, cry sending the grain into waves. Amos wonders what grows at the side of the road and if it would look pretty picked, put in a vase atop the gingham for breakfast.

Field Work

I didn't watch, but knew that you woke up,
tangled in sheets of a bed alone.

The miles a straight shot down I-70, through the Midwest
where highways cross the states like a second nature.

Fields of arching center pivots water the same redundant stalk
    of corn,
as Virginia sprawls its length across the atlas.

On the road any sight of Missouri is lost on I-81 behind apple
    orchards
and the silk of caterpillar nests.

What Bothers Me About Us

We haven't cooked together yet, your meals more often
from Schwan's, wrapped tight in cold plastic.

Your memory and being introduced to Uncle Mike three times,
how it's been four years but you want month anniversaries on
    every ninth.

Our lack of experience with empty bottles, that the only
    refracted light
we know is yellow streaks in the morning bending to wake us.

That I can't write about our relationship, teenage drama
    half of who we are.

How you don't laugh as much as you used to, the constant
chatter of how we're going to raise our unborn children.

I want to know the taste of wine on your lips, if your apple-
    like breath would change
the flavor, if my smoking would bother you.

I want to have been with other women, known the feeling of
    different skins,
the taste of other mouths.

I don't know how to love a woman all the time, only how
    to want her,
like the strain of wanting in a leash.

Imagine if Eve Knew How to Bake

Sin is like breaking apple skin—the crisp chirp
from gnashing teeth to grain
back to bone. If only we were capable of savoring
our vices. Long draws of cigarettes,
drinking our liquor quick, the pinch
is fleeting and the stupor only lasts so long.
Imagine Eve baking that fruit
into a pie, and her and Adam
taking their time to relish every last taste of sin—
lapping pleasure from dish
using finger and tongue,
syrup slipping from loose lips.

Probabilities

1

I imagine Dorothy waking up half-naked,
with skin dried out from two bottles of wine,
the shepherd's pie on the table,
cold as New England homes.
I want to say that unsure steps
down two flights of teasing
stairs are grace, but she is in descent
and the chance of rain is 80%.

2

She dyes her hair red, but the brown
won't go and instead looks more like chestnut,
the broken scales of longleaf pine,
an empty bottle of Southpaw. My hand
meets the cool of glass, mouth a cigarette
and I drag as smoke climbs like Virginia creeper.

3

She is the type that would shimmy.
I wonder how many shakes
it takes to pull jeans over or under
her Terre Haute waist, leftovers
of where the Midwest meets the South.
Where the sweet tea scent of southern summer
is carried out to the Indiana border and the air
smells a bit more like sugar than usual in June.

Ode to Mags

The Sunsphere is the color of my grandmother's teeth,
she is a wickered woman. Her Boomsday voice carries,
each word a kamuro, laugh a crackle. The smell of golden
plackis fill her home. When she cooks, she sings the story
of a Polish girl slaughtering a pig. I like to think
it takes her back to when her hair was black as poppy
seed, skin as white as quark, and her hands ran red
with czernina made from lovers.

Imaginary Waltz with a Woman
Wearing a Dress of Virga

Your silhouette is caught between windows and hanging smoke
thin as muslin, elongated in streaks of vodka tonic
lining the tumbler like a Midwestern storm. I want nor'easters,
the Tennessee gales, the sneaking wind, its creeping cool—
I learned the smell of thunderstorms, cold copper with a hint
of tin, the ground wet before it even starts to rain.

Arrival of the Normandy Train

We talked about our favorite artists—Seurat's stipples of cool color, and how the strokes of Monet are like looking through diner glasses full of tap. The train at Normandy was a prediction, the lack of faces, a hollow station, how everyone was boarding and no one was arriving. The audio guide said the brush imitates the movement of smoke and patrons, but there is no bustle at the stop, only a howl from the last steam engine as the scene goes flat like Coke that the Greeks like to serve. I thought of an artist in the parking lot, painting a new rendition of Hopper's *Nighthawks*, and wondered if his paint strokes would match the distance across the booth as we placed two orders of baklava.

Eulogy for an Imagined Woman

She lies in the bed wearing a white shirt
dyed clear by the sun, the whole of her covered
except what she wants to show.
The scar on her breast, at the apex
of her areola, once red is now the same
faint pale of her body. She is removing her jeans,
cuff stiff at the ankle slides over ink
that stains her feet with dead sparrows.

The bed becomes the shade of apricots,
every crease in the sheet, each ridge
folds towards her, but she looks
away, out the window where the sun sets.
We aren't getting closer and I did not care
about the color of the room or lack
of touch, I didn't care about the arrangement of freckles.

I wanted another girl, and now, it is a dogwood
winter in east Tennessee—the fat irises,
cocooned in ice, in a few days will thaw
and brown. In my bedroom, the light
dyeing the white walls the same shade
of yellow as dead corn,
all the bends of the bed pointing
to where my body slept alone the night before.

Surviving Tennessee Heat

Cigarette stubs line the ashtray
as index and middle fingers wrap the filter
my right hand digs through lint.
Your thumb spins the wheel
as fire starts from flint; lip curls, dragging
smoke to mouth. On the porch, we put
butts out on our childhood.

There was something about the house
you nestled into, the constant smell of char,
rough ridges of hardwood floors.
Our words soaked in whiskey,
like the cherries we ate,
amazed that your tongue
never even touched the spoon.

A Night With Marlowe's Love

The strap drops below Rudi's shoulder, the slip
is slick like the shaft of a sugarcane.
Come, she said, *I'm not sure about the fit
of this negligee.* I lift her up, lay
her across the bed, these sheets of loam and silt.
Cotton skin laid down, she smells of peat—
my hand stalks her shoulder feeling the build
of her body, sweat and satin tastes like leek
or Vidalia. It's the crop of her hair that reminds me to find
the spot my hand belongs—where her hair grows
along the back of her neck like rind
and makes the wave of our bodies slow.
No, Marlowe, she didn't want beetle wing
broaches. What she wanted was free of your myth.

What West May Be

In the west, we didn't know if it was sunset or rise
after staring down saguaros in the Sonoran Desert.
We had seen red dirt all our life but here, earth was burnt
and grown old like bristlecone in White Mountains.

We peeled skin from our hands like strip bark,
made tough as cold leather jackets—

> *God damn,*

you said,

> *look how long this piece of me is.*

The whole of us leaving the sum
of our apple-peel skin.

The Last Night I Was the Person I Thought I Had Always Wanted to Be

In a sense I had become Mara,
wandering the streets of Paris and Amsterdam
narrated in the voice of Benjamin Willard
with the same jungle daze.

In Paris I learned proper ways
to press lips to paper, breathe deeply,
burning all the way down so that the Arc
had its own flare in the absence of light.

Taught how to fuck like a Parisian—
clutch, not coddle,
I remember how the woman said,
être un homme.

By the time I reached Amsterdam
I told prostitutes I was from New York
for important reasons. No one, even whores,
wants to fuck a man from Tennessee.

I tapped a secret
language on a glass door,
my last Euros clenched, suffocating
what life may be in paper money.

I remember the naked honesty of the room.
An empty bed, folded curves
of sheets needing to be familiar,
a light dim enough to hide all the gray.

In that moment,
the trace of acrylic nails felt natural,
the irony of white negligee in this setting.
I paid extra to not take it off myself.

Acknowledgments

"October 2010" was published in *Josephine Quarterly*.

"Imaginary Waltz with a Woman Wearing a Dress of Virga" was published in the *Rappahannock Review*.

"The Last Night I was the Person I Thought I had Always Wanted to Be" was published in *Connotation Press*.

Colophon

Body text and poem titles set in Belwe Std.
Cover text set in Minion Pro.

Christopher Petruccelli is a 2012 graduate of the University of Tennessee. He currently studies biogeography at the University of Missouri and is an associate poetry editor at Stirring. His work has appeared in *Josephine Quarterly*, *Connotation Press*, *Gingerbread House Literary Magazine*, *Rappahannock Review* and *Blast Furnace*. In his free time, Chris chases after things that are bigger on the inside.

Etchings Press

Etchings Press is a student-run publisher at the University of Indianapolis. Each year, student editors choose the Whirling Prize, a post-publication award, in the fall and coordinate a publication contest for one poetry chapbook, one prose chapbook, and one novella in the spring. For more information, please visit etchings.uindy.edu.

Previous winners and publications

Poetry
2019: *As Lovers Always Do* by Marne Wilson
2018: *In the Herald of Improbable Misfortunes* by Robert Campbell
2017: *Uncle Harold's Maxwell House Haggadah* by Danny Caine
2016: *Some Animals* by Kelli Allen
2015: *Velocity of Slugs* by Joey Connelly
2014: *Action at a Distance* by Christopher Petruccelli

Prose
2019: *Dissenting Opinion from the Committee for the Beatitudes* by Marc J. Sheehan (fiction)
2018: *The Forsaken* by Chad V. Broughman (fiction)
2017: *Unravelings* by Sarah Cheshire (memoir)
2016: *Pathetic* by Shannon McLeod (essays)
2015: *Ologies* by Chelsea Biondolillo (essays)
2014: *Static: Stories* by Frederick Pelzer (fiction)

Novella
2019: *Savonne, Not Vonny* by Robin Lee Lovelace
2018: *Edge of the Known Bus Line* by James R. Gapinski
2017: *The Denialist's Almanac of American Plague and Pestilence* by Christopher Mohar
2016: *Followers* by Adam Fleming Petty

www.ingramcontent.com/pod-product-compliance
Lightning Source LLC
Chambersburg PA
CBHW070443010526
44118CB00014B/2174